D1192794

Visits from the Seventh

Visits from the Seventh

■ ■ ■ ■ ■ ■

poems

SARAH ARVIO

ALFRED A. KNOPF

NEW YORK 2002

THIS IS A BORZOI BOOK
PUBLISHED BY ALFRED A. KNOPF

Grateful acknowledgment is made to the following publications,
in which some of these poems first appeared:
The Paris Review: "Floating," "How I Yearn," "Denmark," "Death,"
"A Flower," "Moon Gazing," "Temptation," "Static Interference,"
"Malice," "Rêves d'or," "Hats," "A Leaf," "Murder" and "Ellipses"
Southwest Review: "Clouds" and "O Cult"
Literary Imagination: "Fame" and "Reverence"
Columbia: "Love"
Poetry: "Swimming," "Wonder" and "The Centuries"
Raritan: "Memory," "Côte d'Azur" and "Dancing"

"Floating," "How I Yearn," "Denmark," "Death," "A Flower," "Moon Gazing,"
"Temptation," "Static Interference," "Malice" and "Rêves d'or" won the Bernard F.
Conners Prize for the long poem, and were reprinted in *The Best American Poetry 1998*,
edited by John Hollander (New York: Scribner). "Mirrors" appeared in *The KGB Bar Book
of Poems*, edited by David Lehman (New York: William Morrow). "Swimming," "Wonder"
and "The Centuries" won *Poetry*'s Frederick Bock Prize.

The author also wishes to thank the MacDowell Colony and the Corporation of Yaddo.

Library of Congress Cataloging-in-Publication Data
Arvio, Sarah.
Visits from the seventh : poems / by Sarah Arvio.
p. cm.
ISBN 0-375-41367-7
I. Title
PS3601.R78 V57 2002
811'.6—dc21
2001038226
Manufactured in the United States of America
First Edition

For
Julia

Contents

Second Round

First Round

I

Floating

I said some nonsense or other to them
and they mocked back, "but we're your one design,"
or "you're our one design"—which was it?

The pen slipped and capered on the page,
escorted by ripplings in the atmosphere
like breeze with nothing to blow against.

"We wear no form or figure of our own
—a wisp, a thread, a twig, a shred of smoke—
to tell us from the motions of the air.

We'd love to live in even a bubble,
to wrap around its glossy diaphanous,
reaching and rounding, as slinkily real

as a morning stretch or a dance in a field.
But we know only this air, and memory,
once, or several times, removed and turned,

the pang of a once-had, a maybe-again,
that shifting half-light, our home and habitat,
those hours, soft-toned, windless, that favor passage,

the usual relay of twilights. And,
how often a century? The sun eclipsed,
that 'created' half-light, not dusk or dawn:

us glowing through, our light, our element,
in which we show best, glow best, what we are.
Yesterday some snowflakes slipped through us,

refreshing kisses passing through our heat.
Ah, we wanted to say. If we could have,
we'd have laughed right out from sheer surprise."

And what else? "We've got you to stand for us."
And I have you, I said, to float for me. ∎

II

How I Yearn

I had been missing them very badly,
that day and that day and the next—and yet
the solace they offered was imperfect,

airborne and volatile. I invoked them,
yes, often, in lieu of human contact.
Not that they weren't human, just abstracted

from humanness on the physical plane.
But why had they deserted me? I knew
the answer: for spurning them out of hand.

But where, in that case, did they swirl off to?
Did they rise higher, higher, and vanish
into some upper ether or did they

betrayingly visit someone else who
might at that moment seem more receptive?
Calling them back after a desertion

was never simple: I had to turn my mood
soft, bright, calm and dreamily attentive;
then, after a time, they would slip back in,

one by one, refiguring their spirals
in those inevitable rows of seven.
Would they, I once found the courage to ask,

weave together and net the air for me,
linking and looping their remembered limbs,
to break softly my falling if I fell?

Cradle me, oh cradle me, I whispered.
That was not a service they could do, though.
Life is so complicated for us here,

so troublesome, really, that I wondered
how they found theirs. Did they love it up there
cutting their spirals into cold fronts and

turning somersaults with the storms? Did they
nestle cozy into their troughs of air,
basking in the serene and glossy heights,

the breathtaking vistas of blue-gray seas,
the pink-tinted cloudscapes, the high music—
Or did they, as we do, long for blankets

and warm bodies? So I broached that question
when they came soft-shoeing back in this time.
"No memory, no thought," one lipped to me,

"can stand in for the loss of a life of touch."
Amen, I said, and that's the life I want.
So I brushed the air to be rid of them. ∎

III

Denmark

"But how could you tell him? Never ever
have we allowed—have we intimated—
you should share our visits with anyone."
That's I think the gist of what one said.

"All territories have, never forget,
their own imperatives and covenants,
and the tacit ones. Under the so-called
presumption rule—that's Denmark—we presume

that the broader and deeper sovereignty,
crossing all lines, subsuming all bodies,
aquatic or abstract, will override
interior but lesser requisites."

I wanted to argue that telling him
was not so different from telling myself.
"Oh appeal, appeal, if you must," one said.
"We don't mind a hum, a word, a whisper

now and then, alluding to some other . . .
But outright revelation will only
imperil all that we've done, we and you,
to come to this arrangement—all the hours

at work before dawn in the north country,
the briny, eye-blue Baltic blustering
hard by, the sun rising to never more
than low in the sky, a cold yellow blur

gleaming dull in the iced *fourchettes* of trees."
So, was that all? Was that the sum of it?
Must I then keep mum or suggestive or
throw over all that they had been to me?

"Stay, stay," I happened to hear one murmur.
A song sprang to mind: *"Oh, Copenhagen,*
wonderful . . . salty old Queen of the sea . . ."
(Or some such.) They beamed, for they liked that thought. ∎

IV

A Spring

"Go on," they say and say. But I don't know
how they mean. It seems a matter of joy:
"Go on into it." All right, *pester me,*

I whisper back. I find it best to be
prodded into pleasing sensations. (Those
who've gotten the other kind of scolding

know how hateful it can be.) I've listened,
and tried and tried, but as always, *"the will
is not the way."* (As one so sweetly quipped,

"try forcing a spring to flow.") I guess I
know that now and the knowing is a clue.
"It's just the first in a compendium

of clues no one holds the index to." "Yes."
"A flurry of pure air, then some bubbles,
then a rivulet; the less you tend it,

the more it will rise, redouble and rise,
now a smooth-sliding, cool-flowing river
and sometimes gushing up almost wildly."

"The will is not the way." This was their mot,
as usual not all that practical.
But above all else, I should "reverence

what flows from elsewhere," and "how like water,
springing cool among grass blades, parting them,
rising to the rim of the embankment

and finding the first down-flowing passage."
"The green grass may be just a metaphor,
or also" (laughing now) "a memory.

No, the landscape doesn't determine us:
joy will also flow from mud or rubble."
They gurgled and whispered, "yes, darling, yes." ■

V

Death

Well, the night is blooming. Death may not be
(as the atheists would have it) nothing
at all, but rather (think many of us
who've abandoned god for a sense of god)

a moment to move through, on the other
side of which to find, no one knows, but more
than worms and darkness. For some, a power
almost to speak—although *speak* may not be

the term in the absence of lips, tongue, teeth.
To say. By some means they implant their thoughts
into a person's mind. Mine, for instance.
And thus they go on growing and thriving.

At times they only seem to want to chat
or to make florid gestures, curves and sweeps
and curlicues—*esquisses!* Coy promises
—teases of a vision not to be had;

at others they seem to bud or burst forth
with words pushing to be said, and they nudge
and tickle me to say them for them. They're
working on the matter of openness—

not though, for its own sake, as a value,
but so that I'll be more fertile for them.
Not altogether a noble purpose—
but that depends on the nobility

of the thought they're striving to cultivate.
Doesn't the wish to have one's thought thought of
seem vain, decorative? The lingering
effect of having lived well, maybe, and

not being able to leave it at that.
Always one stroke more to add: another
asterisk, addendum or afterword,
sprig after sprig, petal after petal.

And if their thoughts are fine ones (most seem so
these nights) I don't mind helping them out by
letting them do their thinking in my thoughts.
Petals of promise; calyxes of joy.

I like to fancy them as my teachers;
if they use me well, I may even learn
to use myself. And just now the room fills
with a fragrance of flowers. Or of love—

no, that isn't so. And yet, imagine
a garden, not wild but cultivated,
and richly fragrant. Yes, some spring flowers
turned in a breeze: that fresh, that rapturous. ∎

VI

A Flower

"Which ones?" And here they were, with me again,
slipping gently from this topic to that:
"Those for whom earthly senses are almost

not bearable, for whom a rough voice or
vile smell or small abrasion drawing blood
are racking or still worse. Those are the ones

living on the rim of Death, skirting it,
life being too lush, too real and too rich—
meaning, they're allotted too many nerves."

"And for what? To please themselves, god only knows."
"But you can't have one without the other.
You can't be exquisitely pleasured and

not draw darker data through the senses."
There was the rub. They all laughed. We all laughed.
"And 'we all' know what too much pleasure is.

Or do we? (Paolo and Francesca knew.)"
"The truest blessing to the sensitive
is not to live at all. How can a flower

be tolerated, for instance; maybe
it's too grand also, too great a rapture."
"There are many means of passing across,

including the taking of one's own death—
always a mistake viewed from either side."
"The tragedy of course is multifold,

the ones left behind weeping and helpless,
and the departed who must pass forward
through the stations, not having satisfied

the central moment of a Destiny—
arduous passage." "For the extra-sensed
are tasked, you know, with negotiating

the difficult domain of the Divide."
I was tired then from too many such truths,
so I said good night, and I retreated. ■

VII

Moon Gazing

And here now again: it didn't matter,
or did it, whether life's shifting layers
were "collateral or coterminous";

what was essential was to "look ahead
lightly"—"so very lightly"—and to "fuss
pleasantly over the moment's pleasures"

"without religion and without regret."
For that was all there was. *"Now is ever."*
And with these words, a beam of light streamed in,

a soft moonstripe or a neighboring lamp
through whose shine pranced the palest acrobats,
willful almost wanton and expressing

pure contentment at their own fine fact: *now
is ever.* Wasn't that really the "text
and texture of the higher life"? (This time

not excluding the sex organs.) *High* means
exquisitely sensed or extra-sensed? "Yes."
I've asked them but they haven't told me yet

how they sense without the senses. Oh yes,
the sixth sense, I had forgotten that one.
I feel them humming and clucking gently:

"The sixth is sex, silly. The *seventh* is
our sense, the one we sometimes share with you."
(This was a common but crucial error.)

But how then did they gather theirs of us?
I wanted to know, so I pressed and pressed.
"Some, dear, have talked of seeing through the backs

of mirrors. And so it is, or almost so.
We live—*reside*, that is—on the far side
of the moon, watching it in negative

against the light of the sun. Do you see?
Dark moon in a sea of light. Oh to us
almost as wonderful and less like cheese." ∎

VIII
Temptation

I do know the temptation to beg them
to read me the future or to read me
the present so I can parse the future;

and though they may seem to *clairvoient* my mind,
should I trust them to see someone else's?
If they said, "you are the life of his heart,"

if they hummed, "he is yours, now and ever,"
or, "after this hour, he will come to you,"
what if they visioned there not the true thought

but the self-deceit or the subterfuge
and then sang back those thoughts to me? And I
lived my life led by those misreadings?

And what if I said, as I know I did,
where is he now? And they said back "China"?
What China then? "A China of the mind,

mandarin and yes, multifarious,
where a hex means merely a hexagram,
where a wild goose perching on a bare branch

means barren love." Well, was that our China?
Love that I desire return to me
and the change read, "noblehearted return,"

and return means merely "turning again";
"return from a short distance," read the change.
How far had we gone, how far would we come?

Was that then what our China would be?
"The number of sticks is six, the number
for sex, and thus the number of changing."

"Yes, well, sex *is* a danger to the soul:
it wounds the soul and therefore changes it.
The chaste are always wrong. For sex is change

and change is the essence of everything . . ."
You see? Such mediumistic moments
were fraught with bad turns, missteps and false hopes. ■

IX

Static Interference

This one, for instance, just said (I heard him
through a screen of static or scraping wind—
was it the scratch of the pen on the page?),

"Shun that small soul. Shun that small-natured soul.
Avoid mediocrity at all cost."
This was, yes, "improper interference."

"It's really only the new departures
who want, having just left, to intervene,
driven by the onset of new vision."

And "oh alas, in the time of passage
can they be dissuaded? For they haven't
yet grasped the futility of trying

to spare you your plight, your purpose, your oh
so necessary struggles and strivings.
For without them what would life be? As good . . .

as good as . . ." (here one fumbled and broke off,
mawkishly humming) ". . . oh useless to know . . .
oh love your sweet tears." And into the room

flew the sense of a dark song and a throng
of flutters or rustles—were they whispers
or were they soft wings, oh paler than air,

or merely the sense of the sound of them,
and the sound was as waves lapping, laughing,
the sound was as forests ruffled by wind.

And here now again, urgently pressing:
"Waste your talents on that constricting soul
for the love of a spot of affection?

Do you hope to exalt him? Watch how he
tries to count and control you, watch how he
wants to enclose you." And then this other:

"In time (or out of it), we learn to quell
our frustration, to turn our thoughts elsewhere
(I nearly said 'our minds'—how utterly

we are moved to speak your language to you)
toward the outer worlds. Oh yes, so high-flown
these words I know. But a fact is a fact." ∎

X

Malice

There are ones out there as false as any
(a 42nd Street of the Heavens),
gypsies and fantasists, conmen and creeps:
if you're unbefriended they can steal in

at any hour under any pretext,
wanting you to believe in their goodwill
while secretly witching for your downfall.
They're envious, being those least gifted

or those who mismanaged their gifts in life,
so they can't come around honoring or
answering to honor they don't merit.
But do they ask themselves why not, and work

upwards from there? No. After all that time
cavorting idle across the skyscape,
pink, pellucid and cloud-streaked (that alone
should be enough to arouse them to praise),

and grousing about what they didn't do,
they *want* to see you injured or chagrined,
so they can chortle and vent their failure.
An ever-so-alluring deceiver

is the one who tells you your every dream
as though it were the truth of the future;
meanwhile there you stand in a wash of sweat,
your hopes lifted high only to be dashed,

and hear him later laughing fit to burst
and posturing as thunder or traffic.
They *are* hard to tell by this medium
from the grand and good ones (but how like life!)

because of course they really can't be seen
and that makes telling a difficult task,
so Helen-Keller-like in its demand
for varieties of subtle nuance. ∎

XI

Rêves d'or

"The surest bet is to take no counsel
but to love notions in the mere abstract;
to hear *us* as you would hear anyone,

intrigued by the form of the idea
and maybe the manner of the telling
but never taking it as gospel truth."

"And let's not start now with this silliness
of what-does-it-matter-since-fate-prevails:
for you *do* stand there in the yellow wood

and must choose between two diverging paths,
or many paths diverging from a point,
starting now and moving into ever."

"Most of us never begin to assess
the infinite ways we never followed,
various in essence and variform,

a vast web of eventualities
traced negative on the verso of life:
verging, converging and parting again,

or radiating from a single verb,
never ever to return or to meet."
Was it the yellow of the green spring growth,

was it the yellow of the changing leaves,
of summer sun flaming in foliage
and burning the wishbones of the branches?

Was it the rubbed round of the winter sun
lacquering a glare on the frozen snow,
or was it the yellow Indian silk

I wore the last time you made love to me?
The yellow of piss, the refracted rays
in the nubs of the white angora's eyes,

or the yellow of fear—were those woods fear?
Which yellow was it? It was "all of these."
It was the "yellow of your yellow hair."

But this eludes the question of counsel.
This seems to evade the valence of choice. ■

XII

Clouds

Today they just stopped voicing, all at once,
and then struck up again in a new way,
reminiscent of a distant moment

they wish to remind me they coaxed me through.
Did I mind the switch? Yes, I minded it.
The new tone was so sentimental. Thus:

"Haven't you called us to you, after all?"
"Haven't you needed us in the half-light
of morning, in the gray breach of the day?"

"Haven't you cried to us to come and care?"
"Haven't we sat with you for hour on hour?"
"Didn't we say all the while, *love oh love*?"

"Didn't we loop our names always with love?"
"Oh, yes, we admit it's a bit soapy.
And yet, we will vouch for the truth of it.

Years we waited not far from you, floating;
hoping, hoping for the courage of flowers.
And here they rise in their white-and-green vase,

a cluster of white carnations, long-stemmed:
on each green pole the white flap of a flag,
on each green stick the white puff of a cloud,

each a dream, each a sail on a green string,
a thought as light as a *souffle* of wind,
each an antidote, a contradiction,

of all those many sadder days and ways.
An antidote in the shape of a laugh,
in the form of a word of a white rag . . ."

Then this: "We showed you how to turn and curl,
we visioned you how to see in sevens,
we shaped you in the seven shapes of us."

(I longed to protest that I shaped myself.)
"Not a problem for both are just as true . . ."
"Are we proud of our design? Yes, oh yes." ∎

XIII

Fame

"We know about your revelation now
and do we mind? It was a precaution
for your sake, not for ours. And after all,

what can we lose out here singing alone?
(Together, rather, but far from censure.)
We're beyond that now—beyond all caring

about convention, if not about fame."
"Speak for yourself, darling," another said.
"I craved fame all my life, and don't I still?

But it's best to let the living alone
to enact their own choices, bad or good."
And, "oh, yes, the ways I've found to urge them

to remember me leave an aftertaste . . ."
"Whitman did it, although he must have felt
he was priming his readers to accept

the outré and risqué . . ." "And well he should."
"Yes, but that was before he passed across!"
Oh, and "after a certain day and hour

all that belongs to . . . . . ." (here a pause
for one seemed to prefer not to say "god").
"Please don't forget there's no straight view from here.

We can't simply glance over and size up
the state of our reputations, can we?
Try looking into the slick on the slope

of an airplane's wing when it turns a curve;
try reading your status in the rearview
of a passing car: at the most a glimpse.

Try a pool or try a lake, take a sea.
Take a mirror or take a mind . . ." (Take me.)
But how rare is such an access? "Very."

"And even so, what do we see? At best
only what passes through its medium."
Through my medium, they mean: what I see. ∎

XIV
O Cult

"And as for you, we wanted only to
spare you the ridicule of those who would
use the word *occult* to mean *evil cult*.
It means not *cult* at all but *occluded*—

invisible to the eye—what of it?
Even *cult* means only *adoration*."
"To spare you," one went on, "accusations
of evil or insanity or sham."

And then the pen rolled softly on the page.
"*Sham* is the pretense that you speak for us.
Sham is a fake way to a truer truth.
Evil is a notion nonexistent

in the realm of thought, for thought my love
is never *evil*, despite its ugliness.
Thought is idea, *evil* is the act."
And *insanity?* "Lie down on your back

and count and bless the stars that you can keep
the count: there is no more terrible fate
than a mind whose several elements
will not combine, will not coordinate."

"So like the vast of space," one said, "beyond
the cosmic confines far away out there
in the realm of chaos where planets roll
at wild will and often smash where some stars

rise and others fall at random and some
implode. No, hidden as we are we cling,
as you do, to a sense of hope, a hope
of hope, a hope of sensible order."

"And *adoration* is an attitude
of general adoring, objectless,
or angled toward an object out of sight,
more of adorer than of thing adored." ∎

XV

Love

It was not to them I wanted to speak
but they were the only ones who listened.
Do you think I don't know the truth, I said.

Do you think I don't know the half, I said.
I've had half a life to regret all those
regrettable acts of lovelessness. And

did I think he would follow me through them
whispering encouragement, or hissing
not that! not that! I might have hoped it, yes.

But no one could and no one did. I came
alone; I had myself; a bare self is
bare of persons, for they make us ourselves,

they dress us in ourselves. Hope of a self,
to dress in the person of another.
And someplace, in some other, chosen life,

all rival Pamelas shall be unborn,
all plain, brown-haired girls fingering their pearls
with a factual air of what-makes-sense.

"What a waste of words!" But I saw his eyes,
I saw their wander and their wishfulness.
She thinks she got him but she never did.

She thinks she holds him but she never will.
I have him in his sleeping wish and kiss;
she has his truce and loss, his settlement. ■

XVI

History

In a whisper, one of them said to me:
"Why have you never said to us, *why me?*
Do you take for granted our choosing you?

Do you think that we're your voices and, oh,
of course we choose you, having no other?
Do you still wonder if you made us up?"

I barely recall the beginning now:
one day the pen marked a curl, and the word
read "love" (often a word worth turning to).

Love, who? The name came, and then "Here for you."
The words spooled out. *Oh, is someone?* I said,
life having handed me an unfair share

of such someones. "Yes." How they liked the word,
I noted that. "Yes, yes." And then followed
the moments of years of half-light visits:

a name, a note, a notion, nothing more,
and the words: "love, love, love, love, love, love, love,"
in their reassuring crowds of seven.

I knew they came because I needed them.
I weighed their coming by my need of them.
And yet, their criteria were other:

*"We want nerves strained to the edge of a rip,
nerves studied & soothed & almost salvaged,
each in the hold of its own sensation."*

It sang like a psalm. A pause, and then this:
"We never like to expose this standard
because of all those who might feel prompted

to emulate a pain they never knew,
who might simulate your special status—
not a purpose that sources love or art." ∎

XVII

Reverence

The next night, one put it differently:
"We want reverence and irreverence
in a combination that pleases us:
knowing when to adore, when to subvert . . ."

"Oh, even rhythm likes that principle."
And doesn't love? I said. "Yes, love does too.
It's the little subversions, the teases,
a nip on the neck, a breath by the ear,

that excite us into deeper rhythms . . ."
("Do we stretch a point?") *That* was what there was:
"What pulsed and then what pushed against the pulse,
running under the surface of the day,

a violence but a sweet violence,
the tactile balance of a savage thing,
in the balance of love." *That* balanced it.
("So much wilder when contained in the skin

of a person than riding loose out here.")
And now the pen dipped softly: "Bless your night.
It is not like that of us at all we
who view the burning of imploded stars

who follow the turning of the planets
as though slow around us our blood still flowed.
Bless the blood and bless the man in your arms,
bless the capillaries and bless the cells

for that high heat, that material touch."
And this: "Never reach for sensation or
try for ecstasies. In sex as in art,
success, my dear . . ." The pen stumbled and stopped. ∎

XVIII

Park Avenue

I find a pen in my handbag or I
cadge one from a waiter in some café
(I walk that way almost every day now);

leaning up against the marble siding,
I place its tip on a scrap of paper,
a theater ticket, a credit slip,

even a café napkin, and let go.
They always reveal much muscular joy
at being permitted to have a say,

and the pen loops out, "yes, yes," or, rarely,
a vehement "no." I gather they *view*
through the verso of any reflection,

through the silver medium of mirrors,
through the backs of eyes: picture that café
through the sight of one who walks—not easy!

The mirrored sides of skyscrapers *do* help,
despite eternal problems of dazzle:
scen from this side, a grid of silver panes

phasing from pale to deep as day passes;
visioned from that side, oh very much like
a lighted stage in a dark theater

and on its boards a look at real New York.
I know they also crave intimate views,
so I pause for a glimpse in my compact.

I always feel an access of rapture
to be heeding them out there on the street,
as *their* voice—as the voice of one of them—

removes from the noise of my other thoughts,
a cool transparency, so clean and clear,
a lot like the clearness of clear water,

as of flows, as of a sense of flowing.
At times I almost cry from my strange luck
(these *are* the sort of tears they handle best);

note that unhappiness doesn't please them
any more than it does anyone else,
for they can pass their thoughts most easily

through a light happiness, a levity,
empty and sweet and pleased to be alive,
a walk a day along Park Avenue. ■

XIX

Mirrors

A while later that night they flurried in;
some were humming and laughing nervously.
"Have you assessed the deep indecency

most of you tend to feel at having sex
before the spread of a mirror? As though
another couple were in the room and

couldn't help peering at your pleasure or
peeking in your eyes? Who wouldn't flush red
at the sight of two bodies moving in

rhythm both with each other and with you?"
"But under that blush lies a deeper one—
the subliminal, sublunary sense

of being observed from another sphere."
"Thus the preference for modest mirrors,
hung well above the scene and frame of love,

which enhance the room's depth, yes, but offer
at best an oblique view to a watcher
at a higher vantage." "And note that those

who get a thrill from curling and rolling
before mirrors are voyeurs or else want
to be seen by voyeurs, which amounts to

the same thing: a racy view of others'
raptures or lascivious exposure
of one's own." Now the rills of laughter lulled:

"Despite our pleasure at reacquaintance
with breasts, balls, and lips, it is considered
in cosmic bad taste to show too much sex

to the other side." Is it (I was moved
to ask) nostalgic, tender, even raw
to look in later from a place apart?

Giving a low sigh, one spun and then spoke:
"The convocation of qualms and kisses,
the regrets, the assembly of regrets

for those not loved, for those not loved enough,
and for those who should never have been touched
—what else in this death could be more poignant?—

nothing being left of what might have been
but a half glance through a glaze of silver . . ."
And here one stopped. No, one could not go on. ∎

XX

Flying

One said to me tonight or was it day
or was it the passage between the two,
"It's hard to remember, crossing time zones,

the structure of the hours you left behind.
Are they sleeping or are they eating sweets,
and are they wanting me to phone them now?"

"In the face of technological fact,
even the most seasoned traveler feels
the baffled sense that nowhere else exists."

"It's the moving resistance of the air
as you hurtle too fast against the hours
that stuns the cells and tissues of the brain."

"The dry cabin air, the cramped rows of seats,
the steward passing pillows, pouring drinks,
and the sudden ridges of turbulence . . ."

"Oh yes, the crossing is always a trial,
despite precautions: drink water, don't smoke,
and take measured doses of midday sun,

whether an ordinary business flight
or a prayer at a pleasure altar . . .
for moments or hours the earth out of sight,

the white cumuli dreaming there below,
warm fronts and cold fronts streaming through the sky,
the mesmerizing rose-and-purple glow."

"So did you leave your home à contrecoeur?
Did you leave a life? Did you leave a love?
Are you out here looking for another?

Some want so much to cross, to go away,
somewhere anywhere & begin again,
others can't endure the separation . . ."

One night, the skyline as I left New York
was a garden of neon flowerbursts—
the celebration of a history. ∎

XXI

Swimming

"Our relation to you is the same as
that between abstraction and metaphor,
between the idea of a clear lake

and the citing of the lake to describe
the clear idea," one said with a laugh.
Oh, I said then, what a fine idea

and now what lake will embody its fact?
And this: Aren't we tired of comparisons
to the natural world? Then this: "And what

world isn't natural?" "Only the world
of the mind is unnatural." And this:
"It defies nature and defines nature

and won't be defined. The *life* of the mind."
"But its death?" one punned: "Perish the thought."
"In the deep all these questions sink away,

and only the swimming matters: water
sliding around the head and heart and hip,
arms cresting and curving, *with* not against;

carried along on the roll and the rush,
a good swimmer knows water won't resist,
swift or even slow but yes, effortless."

"Are these words merely pretty? No, my dear.
Water is the principle of pleasure
and of pain, the receiver of the touch,

for the cells and tissues are waterbound."
With the splash of a smile one turned to me:
"What bodies do we choose? A glacial lake,

cold as ice, aqua-blue and vaporing,
on which one red leaf is a gash of joy,
a sultry southern sea warm as a bath

and carrying its weight in liquid salt.
We covet water through which light will ride
and you, my dear . . ." Here the words drifted off. ■

XXII

Wonder

What makes the inside of a glacier blue?
—As aqua-blue as any southern sea—
The right color visioned in the wrong place,

the wrong color imaged in the right place,
where wrong is somehow exquisitely right.
Swimming-pool blue looked at underwater

by a swimmer deep down on a hot day,
nuanced like the flows of flowing water
and frozen there inside a flow of ice.

"God is Genius." This was the final truth.
And "genius is the ice and fire of art."
"Art makes now a moment touching *ever*

and makes *ever* a moment touching now."
But whence derives this blue without a source,
essence of evergreen and robin's egg,

as clear as clean water, as clean and clear,
carrying not a needle or a shell,
far and away above the forest line

on a day gray as a field of moraine?
"Oh, it's just as well we can't *really* know,
for knowing would spoil that sense of wonder

so essential to life and love and art.
We must feel there's always more to be known!"
"And of course that's never *not* true, except

in bad art, which puts an end to wonder."
One thought that twist of thought was so clever
(neglecting to add "bad love" and "bad life").

"Yes, god is Genius. But we all know that.
Why make so much of an obvious truth?"
"—The obvious is easy to forget." ∎

XXIII

The Centuries

"The centuries are gone. There are no more.
The world is dead. But don't grieve for too long.
There's another world always on its heels."

"We've had a good run, nothing to scoff at!"
"We must try to count and keep our blessings!"
"Where oh where shall we put *Paradise Lost*

while we fight our final atomic war?"
"That threat's over!" "It has only begun!"
"But where oh where will all the fine words go?"

"—Repair to the planet of higher thoughts."
"—And the trash will lift off and spin away,
caught in the orbit of a lesser star."

"And where oh where shall we lodge the *Nocturnes*
while we forfeit the material world?"
"Oh hang them in air, a fest of pure sound,

suspend them from a moonbeam, from a star!"
"What a day. What a night. Riding the sky
from tune to tune perusing sonatas . . .

And switching then to *Rubber Soul* (why not?)."
"—A high hymnal of the highest order.
There's acoustic room for them all out there."

"But that's just the trouble. Won't they get lost
in the vast space?" "And yet how beautiful:
Picture *Venus de Milo* on Venus

standing oh alone in an abstract beam
of sourceless light. Viewable by the few
out under the stars far from the dull horde

parading glassy-eyed through marble halls . . .
by some few of the many called who have
passed across weeping to our side." "Or by

none viewable by none by none," one said.
"Death isn't sad but the end of life is.
For without your life can we have our death?" ∎

XXIV

Blind Date

"A date with life is a blind date with death."
"Oh but a date with life is also blind."
So who, I said then, makes the bitter choice?

"Do you picture *us* up here at the wheel?
We've never met the Driver either, dear."
"But in all events, this is our advice:

Wear fine underthings in the street. You *can't*
cross wearing tatty lace or torn nylons.
Naked is better! For who ever knows

the moment the method the medium."
"Oh dress well to meet your Match and Maker.
'Clothes make the man!' (*we* paraphrase Shakespeare)."

"Your last mirror may well be a rearview,
a compact, a cruiser, a glint of chrome
on a bathroom floor or on a bumper."

"—Though some prefer the mirror of a lake,
the hues and phases of a lake or sea."
Then one laughing began to lullaby:

"How do you seem in silver blue or glow
in glints of green or bloom in muddy brown
or blush in sunset rose or feel in fog?"

"Yes, always travel in your best attire,
inner and outer (both garter and gloves),
and never flash a ragged fingernail

at a gliding boat or a cruising car
(for the Dead have their own deadly standards)."
"Wear a summer moon wear a silver star

a gleam a glint of frost a fleck of dew
a glowwood glare sport moonrays in your hair."
"No, never forget who and where you are." ■

XXV
Poison Apples

"Love you to death," one said tonight. Such grand
promises. And will you love me after?
"I will love you even ever after."

A comfort abstract but no less complete.
It was far better it then seemed to me
to be loved in the dark by some unknown

—some virtual or relative unknown—
with ideal awe and miscomprehension
than to be loved as who I am and was,

for real, in all my real and rich detail,
who ate the rosy halves of several
poison apples from the hand of the Queen.

". . . Yes, those who live best live in make-believe . . ."
". . . to live well is to play it well, yes, yes . . ."
". . . where believing is almost becoming . . ."

". . . at our best in perpetual low light . . ."
But all Blanche's low lights and pure desires,
no, could never make her Snow White again

despite the fairest mirror on the wall
for the poor fair girl got lost in the Wood
and turned then to the kindness of strangers.

"Love us oh love us," one said, "if you will."
It would be a devotion of the kind
"reserved for gods" or—who knew?—"for angels."

And just then I saw that the red of dawn
had lacquered the boughs of the apple trees
and painted a blush on the frozen snow. ■

XXVI

Motherlessness

"We're referring to those with primal holes,
those whose souls were improperly sutured
in that so delicate time after birth

when the soul is as fragile as the skull
and calls for a mother's tender stitches . . ."
"No, of course we mean to say 'anyone's.'"

"Leaving a hole in the skin of the soul,
a hole in the soul that should be a whole
(yes, please forgive this tired old homonym)

or several holes out of which it leaks . . ."
"So even the sparest nuance of wind
is a feeling, and in cases like those,

can you conceive of a sexual touch?"
"The mothered ones seldom consider how
they simply breathe the boon of love and blood;

those are the lucky ones, with whole smooth skins
like the spandex bodyskins of dancers.
The unmothered—no sooner do they sew

one gap shut than another hole opens,
for the fabric is fragile or brittle
and the person inside keeps pushing out

(the mere movement of life pushes or pumps)."
"Can you dance in a bag? Dance in a rag?
Are you living, darling, or are you dead?"

So what can be done for the sad unsewn
whose souls opened at birth but never shut?
Reluctantly, one murmured a reply:

"Oh weep, weep for them, for the leaking ones.
How close they really come in life to death . . ."
"All the looseness but not the liberty." ∎

XXVII

Memory

"And do we remember our living lives?"
Did I remember the clock or the door,
or the words "I love you" or the word "why";
did he recall the blue vein in my wrist
or only the ice-blue burn in my eye?

What remained of the room and of the night,
the kiss or the argument that ensued?
"You see, our memories are much like yours,
here a shadow, a sound, a shred, a wisp . . ."
"And do we want to remember?" one said.

"Never never Oh give me the blurred wish
or the dream or the fact half-forgotten,
the leaf in the book but not the read page,
not what I saw but what I felt I saw,
not what I felt but how I wished to feel,

give me what I can bear to know I felt."
I choose to recall only the blue dusk.
"Do you think you choose? If only you could
determine your secret determinants."
Did I recall the cocktail as it smashed

against the wall there, so close to my eye,
did I forget why I left my home, why?
The full events of that terrible time
dissolving into the deep hues of dusk
and leaving essence to the inner eye. ∎

XXVIII
Library

"We stick to our guns more than others do,
meaning that when we say *love* we mean *love*,
and aren't apt to distort the nuances . . ."

"Although we acknowledge that all truths shift,
we know how to tell a truth from a fact.
A truth that is *stated* becomes a fact."

Had I hoped to persuade him to believe
I never said those words that night to him?
"The written word lasts best," one said. "'*My Life*

had stood—a Loaded Gun—' is a fact that
can't alter." And then one: "Oh remember
the library at Alexandria

where centuries of words went up in smoke."
I was gunning down the road, wild with grief
after they told me he had shot himself.

Was it because I had withdrawn my love?
Here lay a fired gun that couldn't retract,
although it longed to deny its bullet

in the acrid afterlife of that blast.
Is there a room where all the bullets go
after firing to rest and grease their blaze?

"Yes, a library lined with oily stacks
of cartridges cradling their lost bullets
whose shot truths are the *statement* of a fact." ■

XXIX
Côte d'Azur

Out of the blue, one of them lipped to me:
"A handful of days can hold a whole life,
sunlight dazzling on a blue foaming sea,

the touch of a body and nothing more,
one whisper which was the very whisper
for which you had waited hour after hour,

maybe not the same words, not the same voice,
all those words other and voice still other,
the ring of unknown words, those were the ones."

The hand that held my pen began to shine:
"How sad are those who borrow their solace
from several days never to return,

some incident of passion or promise,
some glimpse . . ." "Oh yes, but sadder still are those
who never bask on even that brief beach."

How blue the sea looked; it shone and *they* shone;
now they glittered with an utter glitter,
now they beamed, for this was their greatest *yes*.

"The special few are those who live full joys,
not a day, a week or a mooncycle
but an extension of years, or a life."

"Chimera on the surface of the sea,
haze that lies heavy on a salty sea,
haze hovering over a summer sea,

despite the scintillations of the sun."
"Where will all this lead? It will lead *nowhere.*
Nowhere at all is where we want to go.

A blue *nowhere* made up of blue nothing,
a moment of bliss lasting a moment,
long enough for life, that long and no more." ∎

XXX

Dancing

"What's the underside of scintillation?"
"Drops of deeper darkness curling like ink
on a dark page," one said. "Scribbles of ink . . .

A dark discotheque where the dated strobe
sends out curling rays of a darker dark.
And the sound is the underscore of sound,

beating unheard like the thrum of your heart . . ."
He dreamed he found me at a club downstairs
on Upper Park. I was dancing alone

in a slinky low-cut black cocktail dress
on whose black *sequins* photographs were pinned,
showing "sequences" from our shared past life,

in black and white. *Oh rescue me*, I said.
That was not my wish but his dreamed desire
to answer when I called this once for all.

If that was the dream, what had been the life?
And here again always: *"Now is ever."*
"Do we have *ever*? Yes, we have it too.

We have only this night, only this day,
& then one more night & one more day."
And then will we know? "The signs point to *no*." ∎

XXXI
Wish

"THE MYTH OF ULTIMATE SATISFACTION
V. THE KINGDOM OF HEAVEN ON EARTH
where the enactment of imagined life

shall be the only final Testament.
Against a heritage of chromosomes,
be HARUSPEX and be EXECUTRIX."

"What do we testify?" "The word of law."
"Have it foretold and told." (One almost wept.)
"Inscribe it on the corpus of the life."

"As for the Will, call it *wish* or *desire*.
There were no *humors, spleen* or *elements*
in those days either; now there is no *will*.

Only pure action and pure energy
enabled by the signing of the Wish,
some action enabled, some action stopped."

"The wish that falls, the wish that floats or flies,
the wisher in possession of the Wish."
"Yes, an agreement among known Parties,

or the parts of the body politic,
or between your State and an unknown one."
"*Annex:* 'Your life shall be your very own.'

Done at such and such a place *WHEREVER*,
in the year of our Love *X X X X*."
And here they kissed and [*signed*] the document. ∎

Second Round

XXXII

A Well

For a year I had tried to shake them off
but then found I had only left myself,
"high and dry"— dry, without a source. Had I

hoped their words rose from my own source, my well?
"But all the voices rise from 'somewhere else' . . .
A 'new' voice can be shrill and thin, but one

that has flo–flowed . . ." (the word came drifting up)
"through sev-er-al ve-ssels" (what did one mean?)
"is res-on-ant re-si-du-al and real."

(I heard my father laughing: "Well, well, well . . .")
"Yes, we like an 'old' voice or a torrent
a chorus welling washing through one pipe

all at once through one throat in a temple
yes *a cappella* singing as though one."
At last the words rose through me "swimmingly."

It was not a question of "former lives"
or of "future lives," since *"now is ever."*
As always it was "water and the sense

of water a teardrop a pane of glass
a glass half full or . . ." Here one swallowed hard.
"All clear, cross-lucent or clairvoyant things,

all things that waver or that well like waves,
all things through which some 'other' shines or shows . . ."
And now the gurgle of a silly song:

"Fear tears pour cold from the middles of eyes
Joy tears are warm & slip from the corners
Anguish tears are salty & scald the cheeks

But love tears pool & glisten in the lids."
The mirror flattened; the room was glazed and soft.
We were "one" again. I had sourced myself. ∎

XXXIII
Waiting

"What's the heaviest word in the language?"
"Wait." "Oh, but *want* is heavier than *wait*."
"But *want* with *wait* is even heavier."

"What's the lightest word?" *"Wit, white."* "A white fence,
a white page, a cloud . . ." "The white of an egg,
the white of an eye . . ." "The wink of an eye

is as heavy as *white* . . ." "White of wisdom,
white of wit." There's dark wisdom too. "Yes, yes."
I went to bed; I waited in the dark.

"How long did you wait?" I waited, I said.
"Oh, how long will you wait?" I'll wait, I said.
"A wanton wish, or an unwonted want?"

"A dark wish. *Want* is the work of the heart."
In my dream, I weathered a "wall of wind."
Wall-eyed and wallflower, well of tears, wall.

"But *wait* can also be the lightest word."
"Wait with *wish?"* "With the wisp of a wish or
worlds of wishfulness." Though what's in a word?

"Are you waiting for a weather report?"
"The weather of desire? The famous wings?"
Not "the wings of . . . ," but "waiting in the wings."

"Some like a whistle, some want a wave,
some like a window, some like a whip,
some want words, some like wind & water." ∎

XXXIV
Lilies

Then I heard a laugh. "We've lived many lives."
"Those who remember them are lost in life."
"Do you loathe lilies? The scent of perfume

on the day of your shame in 1201.
Do you despise the taste of caraway?
They plied you with aquavit till you 'sang.'

Do you hate pork? There was nothing but pig
and cabbage the winter of 405."
"The most memorious are the most mad."

"Mad ones revisit their ancient troubles."
"Mad ones relive their former tragedies."
But is there a cure, I wanted to know.

"There is no cure—the cure was 'love at birth.'"
"Birth love seals the vestigial memories."
Now is "late in the day." Now is "too late."

"Sad fact." "Sorry, sorry," more than one said.
"But you," one argued, "have been soothed and spared."
The pig and the lily are "just a hint."

"Lilies that fester," another said this.
Caraway: "*Swing low,*" one began to sing.
"*Carry me away on the Waters of Life* . . .

Who blushed for you as the calyxes fell?
Who kissed your toes as she emptied the flask?
Who held the scented hankie to your nose?" ∎

XXXV
Yes

Every now and then one would blurt out *yes!*
A splurt of a *yes,* or a small *hurrah.*
What did I want? A "reverie a day,"
a "flag," a "flower," a "flock of hellos"?

Did I expect "bliss"? Did I, did I? *Yes.*
I longed for the river of what they were
to flow through the channel of what I was.
"And say what?" one said. "We've said it *all.*

We've given you a century, a day . . ."
A flag flapping, the crowd cheering, bright light
rebounding off the flagpole; rising wind,
a heart lifting full of old-fashioned hope,

a halo, first gold, now made of rainbows.
So was there a choice? Could I choose my hat,
my hope? The crowd roared and tossed its halos.
The air shone and sparked with spinning prisms.

Was there a "choice that lay behind the choice"
I "seemed to have chosen" but "never chose"?
Was it both "prismatic" and "pragmatic,"
would it "outlast the recent century,"

and was the reverie "reverential,"
what was the "river," and *which* was the "bed,"
and *which* day in *which* century would keep?
(The wind flagged as the dusk began to sift.)

The essential choice was "the sense of choice,"
the essential sense was "the hat and hope."
"Are you in yourself when we are in you,
& who are you within when we are you?" ∎

XXXVI

It

"We mean we never had a word to say."
It was the sound of the word they liked or
if not the "word" then the "flow of the words"

"flowing together, petal by petal,"
as though they carried the "flux of a life"—
the "stream that flows through us when we feel touched."

"Remember that day, the day of his death,
the 'lady of god,' yes, when she touched you
a stream of cool water slipped through her hands?"

Yes? "She did not say Jesus or Buddha . . ."
(Though "what's in a name?") "No, she did not say
you may call him what you will, call him *It*."

What was that sense? "It was the sense of *It*,
meaning the sense of nothing with a name
that you would never give for nothingness."

"A sort of *It*, not sex, not secret love,
not cultish love: the rose of creation."
"Just the concentrated flow of a force,

and the sense of fragrance without a smell,
the sense of a flavor without a taste."
"The elixir of concentrated life."

"A sound like a voice, one of those voices
you could breathe or eat, a voice you could kiss."
And what was the essence of having *It*?

"Our cool glow, our golden rose, our halo,
our sun as dark gold as gold leaf. Our It."
That was the day he died, he had gotten

It. "Our word so late in the day, our *It.*
A word, whatever word, it says *It It*
our word it says what it will, it says *It.*" ∎

XXXVII

Hats

"Oh, how we love the glow of holy gold!"
They curled, cavorting in the evening sun.
"Oh, but centuries have passed since the rage
for halos." "Yes, they're out of fashion now."

"The angels have departed, and auras
may now be had and read in many hues."
"Some see the shine on the heads of others,
others read luminations in themselves."

"Yes, now we have the hues of bliss and wit,
and awkwardness and intuition, yes . . ."
I saw a violet sign that shone and hissed;
it gleamed like neon in the dropping dusk.

I had wished for a tender poets' blue,
but here was the hue of enlightenment.
The sign scrolled out *NARAN*, my spirit name.
"Why wish," one turned and hissed, "why wish, why wish?"

It was gentian blue; it was indigo;
it was myrtle or mauve, a rose-blue vein;
the silver blue of oysters on the half;
ink smeared thin across a violet sky.

It was a distillate of Dusk, a sign
that I was seeing and that I was seen.
"What's the fashion in hats?" "No hat at all."
"Oh, stylists try, but hats just don't come back!"

"And those who like to read luminations
do so on bare or bald or hatted heads."
"Mad as hatters, we love the hidden hues!"
"Yes, the seventh sense is *also* color." ∎

XXXVIII

A Leaf

ADDRESS ME, I said, and I meant "please speak."
"Oh you mean *UNDRESS ME*," one said and turned.
Had I meant "take off my dress"? "What," said one,

"is your address?" My dress was green as moss,
as pine, as weed, as seafoam, as a leaf.
What did I say? I said *GREEN AS A LEAF*

not *GREEN AS BELIEF*. Belief was "a leaf
no one should wear." "Take off belief and wear
a dress." Belief was "no address at all."

"Undress & address your audience."
YES, UNDER DURESS I HAVE BEEN UNDRESSED.
I SAW THE LEAVES BECOME A NEST OF SNAKES;

I WATCHED THE SNAKES ENACT A SWARM OF HANDS.
Was there a sign on a blown-over leaf,
was there some inner palmistry or plan?

Here was a question "not to be undressed."
There was nothing to do but to revert
to a state of address before belief.

Here was the hand, the *feuille effacée.*
"Turn a new leaf," one said, "and turn a cheek.
Shed leaves, shed tears. *REDRESS YOURSELF.*" ∎

XXXIX

A Pea

Late one green night. Now me: Like the princess,
I bruise as I ride on the pea-green sea.
"It was a pea-green boat," one said. "The fog

is thick as . . . soup." "You're splitting . . . *never mind.*"
(The puns were flying now.) "But is there *peace*
or *appeasement?*" Then this: "No, only peas,

and on a rare night, green cheese." Now one droned:
"We like pale cheesy green, despite the face
owling in the dark . . . we like earthen &

unearthly greens: leaves, moss, emeralds,
seaweed . . . green stars, green peas . . . the princess
bowing in her green gown & grinning CHEESE.*"*

And this: "We never meant to go to sea."
"Chlorophyll and oxygen, our favorite foods."
There wasn't much peace as we spooned up soup.

"Do you want some advice?" one (sipping) said.
"Emulate the traits of pussies and owls."
Four-footed and wingèd? "No, lovable

and wise." What about the princess? I said.
Did the pea make her arrogant and mean?
Did the pea make her hate the life she lived?

With time, she had learned "not to blame the pea
for her nervous vulnerability . . ."
"or the mattress" . . . and to "bruise gracefully." ∎

XL

Garden

One crooned in my ear; I was waking up.
"Why insist that Eden was a Garden
with an apple, a lady and a snake?"

Then one: "Snow White bit an apple and blushed
to death." Then one: "Not the apple-a-day-
that-keeps-the-doctor-away." And: "The snake

was a garden worm in her mother's eye."
Her eye was a garden? I said and smirked.
"Any eye is Eden or a Desert."

"Yes, the difference is a *UNIVERSE*."
"Though a *verse* is a *turn*," one (tartly) said,
"*return*, you'll note, has never meant *reverse*."

"Can she go back & eat the yellow half?
Can she go back & never eat at all?
Can she turn the dark Queen into Glinda

with a click of red heels & a blown kiss?"
No, not in all the "versicles of hope"
if "seven little men" had "tried and failed."

And this was the "meaning" of *UNIVERSE:*
"one-turn-forward and there's-no-going-back."
And return is "always a compromise,"

like "go home to Eden and wear a dress."
Or only in the mirror on the wall
in which she lives "the fairest life of all." ∎

XLI

Murder

"Oh, murder!" she was heard to mutter, or
"Mary mother of god!" You see how close
these utterances come? Please *kiss me* Mom.

"Dial M for melancholy." (Pity me.)
"Dial M for misery & M for muse."
Of the several choices, I choose muse,

though I'd like an evening with Ray Milland,
the kind of murderer most girls desire,
the kind of *kill me* we might murder for.

"You know *mutter* is a word for *mother*
whereas *murmur* might be a mom we want."
"Are you dying, dear, for a cup of milk?"

"Dial M for the milk of mother's love."
"What other milk, we ask, is such a must?"
"An M won't buy you whiskey or water."

"*Dial M for Medea*, who butchered her
babies to settle a score with their dad."
I'd rather dial M for Ray Milland.

"Isn't that the point? So would she, my dear.
(May we remind you, hell hath no fury.)"
Was that the murder motive, jealousy?

Dial M for me & M for what I am,
a girl with no mother to dial for.
A girl whose mother was her murderer. ∎

XLII

Dreamorama

"Dream yr dreams," one said. "Silly, isn't it?
Most think this means *fulfill yr ambitions.*
Wrong! It means *dream yr dire, exotic dreams . . .*"

"Here's a new technotherapy," one said.
"Scan yr mind's eye view for doctors and friends."
"Not enough RAM to store the stuff in yr

mind? Store yr overflow in cyberspace."
"Not enough time for precious R.E.M.?
Store contents, view later." Now another:

"Oh, still at issue: how to avoid dream
data fragmentation during transfer . . ."
"*HEAD*line of the morning *ETHERPAPER:*

ANOTHER DREAM DOSSIER BURSTS, SCATTERS"
Images tumble through the outer space,
"diving" and "tripping" over the airwaves,

"full-formed" or "fragmented" or "disfigured,"
"gaudy or gleaming, pastel or grayed-out."
The outer space scrambles with inner space . . .

"A TOE SOME TRASH A TOADSTOOL A TATTER
TREACHERY A TREAT A TREATISE A THREAT"
"*Night flowers flying on the wanton wind.*"

They thought they were funny. Were they funny?
"A DRAM A DRUG SOME DROOL A BIT OF DIRT
A DRAMA DELIRIUM DREAD A DRAG

A DALLIANCE A DEATH A DART A DIG"
"Don't like yr images? Re-envisage.
Faller, flyer? Revamp yr inner arc.

Don't dig the feeling? Redesign the frame."
"Ha," one said, "a dream beyond ambition:
reconfigure yr DRAMAS & TRAUMAS." ∎

XLIII

Moon Song

Once we met on a night without a moon.
"You don't need a moon to feel the longing,"
one said. "All earthly matter is moonstruck.

Aren't we all moon-babies? Aren't all earthlings
moon-mavens?" And then this: "Our most human
feature is mooning." But what about dogs,

I said. Don't dogs moon? "No, dogs *bay* at moons."
"*Stare, stare at the cold green face of the moon.*
Why, there's nothing there, no grass, no trees,

and certainly no cheese . . ." "That goes unsaid."
"We gaze toward Otherness, as in 'the grass
is always greener on the other side.'"

"Mooners that we are our fate is lunar."
(They like a rhythm, they like a rhyme.) Why?
"Because complacency is a fat cow

chewing grass as it lows in a meadow."
"Going to the moon won't get us our moon,
no thank you, Mr. Glenn, any more than

surgery will cure heartache." And then this:
"Oh leave us our golden calves and moon songs."
And now seven slipped shining into song:

"*You've seen a blood-red moon, you've seen it green,
you've seen it white as ice and ringed in mist,
a gray face floating on a rosy sea.
Have you seen a blue moon? I saw one 'once.'
I saw a yellow moon* out of the blue." ■

XLIV

Three Green Stars

Was it an admission of arrogance
to say right out that I had visitors?
We were driving in the Jersey meadows,

a gray purple sky, roving orange spots,
white clouds lit miasmic yellow. "It might
be best," one said, "to call us a conceit."

The road flares rayed; the dotted lines spun smooth.
Another: "Arrogance is like conceit."
"Knowing of the movements of molecules,

who dreams that what you see is what you get?"
"No, what you see is never what you get."
Another: *"Seeing isn't believing—*

and *out of sight* is never *out of mind."*
"It's arrogant to reduce the wonders
of the universe to the size of your

sciences and fictions." A sigh, a cough.
Three green stars frisked on the skyline. And then:
"What *crank* called this chaos a *UNIVERSE*?

"*One turn* of a wheel? *One turn* of a thought?"
"At the helm of a roving Satellite,
a hand on a handle is *cranking* out

electrons, monads, endorphins & mist,
duendes & dreams, quarks, quirks,
ions & eons, beams & rays,

atoms & daimons, spots & dots."
"Be humble," one mewed. I hung to the wheel.
"Matter or not, it's all material." ∎

XLV
Cake

"Since notions are what they are, never wrong
and never right, as long as they're notions,
though most still court what we call *conviction*,

our only counsel, dear, is *Live by none*."
One wet her lips. "Those who embrace received
religions and old ideas are servants

of dead queens and lords, sucking on wafers
when they could have their cake and eat it too."
"Oh browse at the table sighing with sweets,

with cake & berries & sweet sparkling wine."
"Amen," one said, "for lovers of sweetness,
sweet tooth will always be the highest praise . . .

Compare *sour grapes* and *half-baked opinions*."
It was time for an ideology
of the "sumptuous and edible" truths:

This tastes This feels This is . . . They didn't mean
Dr. Williams' plums. They meant: *"Oh savor
Eternity in a forkful of cake."*

They didn't mean "sweets to the sweet," oh no.
Now a smile and a smack of lips. They meant
Marie Antoinette had a "nice notion"

though it was also one that "cost a neck."
*"Oh shun conviction & eat confections.
Give us . . . give us this day our daily cake."* ■

XLVI
Yvoire

We'd been at Yvoire on the other shore,
where the lake mirrored a "tender" pink sky:
two plates of filet, a flask of pink wine,

a rag of pink cloud, a ribbon of wind . . .
"Pink," one said, "is still the color of love."
Was this "simile" or "syllogism"?

These were "unlike things alike in color."
"Oh cultivate softness & subversion.
Oh succor sensuality & fact."

What fact? I asked. What facet of a fact?
"Oh, love his girlish shame and his pink cock,
love his pink nipples, the scar on his cheek."

The "symmetry" is the "synecdoche,"
part for a whole as in *sail for a ship*,
where the pink evening and the pink filets

are the "emblems of a sensual fact."
What faction or refraction of a fact?
"The heart," one said, "is the throne of all joy."

"It's a muscle," one said, "a piece of meat."
Was one facetious? Here was the refrain:
"Is there juice, is there joy & jouissance,

is there manna & music & money?"
Could I face him and could I face myself?
"Oh, facsimile is as real as fact." ∎

XLVII
Shangri-la

"Abortion, so what? Souls shed like old skin.
A moment later, one might have attached
to a Sherpa—a Sinbad—a Shiva—

a Scheherazade—" Why all the *shhhhs*?
"For the hush that ushers in the choice."
We'd been climbing all day in nipping cold.

"Some are dry and yellow like old paper,
some are sweet and damp like cherry petals."
"As molecules move, thus do souls." "—As sperm,

as atoms—remember your Lucretius . . ."
"And none is worth a shred, a scrap, a jot
until one sticks . . ." The air was cold and sharp.

"When the story begins, it must resolve . . ."
"A universal law." ("A *flaw*," one hissed.)
"If one sticks too long, the story begins,

and then *grief to all* on letting go." "No,
there's nothing holy in a particle."
"What about the Uterus it clings to?"

"And a condom—wouldn't that have helped?"
I wonder if I wouldn't have preferred,
in my life, I said, some other Hostess.

"Hush," one said, "there is no Preferment."
We had come to Shangri-la: falling snow,
medallions of frost and ash, glassy tears,

dewstars and dustflakes and cherry petals
clinging and melting on the mountainside.
O Confetti of our "created" world. ■

XLVIII

A Bug

Hot late summer: the dry leaves made no sound.
The only sound was the step of a foot
on the porch boards and then a shout: "WE DON'T

EAT BUGS!" The baby wept, the baby screamed.
And then: "SPIT THAT OUT!" The bug lay vicious
on her tiny tongue. Yes, the bug had juice,

the bug had love. But to make the bug love
her was the work of years. A small voice said,
"Turn it to gold and let it fly." And yet

a century crept by before the bug
turned to gold. A hot sun *jaundiced* the porch,
the trees, board by board and leaf by leaf. Or

was the word *burnish?* Did it *burnish* them?
So that her rankest thoughts by turning gold
"became" her, or beautified her as she

became. She knew the phrase "a heart of gold,"
but other organs could be golden too.
"To a Flying enemy make a Bridge

of Gold." One said that long ago, but make
your enemy into a golden bridge?
So late, a sense of what might matter and

what shouldn't; a place where a ring, a glint,
a tuft of blond hair, the rim of a cloud,
a gold leaf, a bottle cap all bask in

the damasked memory of the golden forms;
where all things and thoughts show how well she glows.
By now the bug had flown; so had the years. ∎

XLIX
Ellipses

Why was a *sole* an *only* and a *foot?*
And why was *soul* not *solar,* not *solid?*
Alone I was "yes, a solipsism,"
lips stammering alone (do you read that?);

I opened my lips, hoping one would speak.
As always they "preferred the passages"
between "no and yes," between "dark and bright,"
"those rays of the sun from behind the earth,"

never the "eye of the sun," its "sham truths,"
its illusion of "seeing all." They loved
all verges, the Dusk, the Dawn, the dusky
grays, the grayed and shadowed hues, all shadows

and ellipses (here were my lips again),
lulls, lapses, what was lost or left unsaid
or stated elsewhere; leaps of faith and love,
love, leaps of love, lips (read mine, I said),

the gentle attraction of gravity,
gradations and degrees, stairwells and steps,
hallways, hellos, and even some farewells:
all that led elsewhere and was else than self;

the object not the subject, the other
not the one. They endorsed Desire, this was
their Desideratum, *ipso facto*
(could these be lips again? read mine, I said);

all things "through which some other showed or glowed."
They loved "a shingle hanging on a door,"
a shiver, a sheer dress, a burst of song,
two shadows overlapping on a wall;

all things that "transited toward Otherness,"
"transitional, translucent, in a trance";
desire "because it tended somewhere else."
They "shunned all certainties and forecasts"

(in this they were like me; we shared these thoughts);
nothing was known, this they were sure they knew;
and "if anyone knew," it might be them.
The sun was eyeing us; I lapsed and slept. ■

A NOTE ABOUT THE AUTHOR

Sarah Arvio was born in 1954 and grew up near New York City. Educated at schools abroad and at Columbia University, she now works as a translator for the United Nations in New York and Switzerland.

A NOTE ON THE TYPE

The text of this book was set in Van Dijck, a modern revival of a type-face attributed to the Dutch master punch cutter Christoffel van Dyck, c. 1606–69. The revival was produced by the Monotype Corporation in 1937–38 with the assistance, and perhaps over the objection, of the Dutch typographer Jan van Krimpen. Never in wide use, Monotype Van Dijck nonetheless has the familiar and comfortable qualities of the types of William Caslon, who used the original Van Dijck as the model for his famous type.

Composed by NK Graphics, Keene, New Hampshire

Printed and bound by Edward Brothers, Ann Arbor, Michigan

Designed by Soonyoung Kwon